# WALKS AROUND WHITBY

## 10 WALKS UNDER 6 MILES

**Dalesman**

First published in 1999 by Dalesman
*an imprint of*
Country Publications Ltd
The Water Mill, Broughton Hall,
Skipton, North Yorkshire BD23 3AG

Reprinted 2005

Illustrations © Christine Isherwood:
p5, harebells; p8, pelican's foot shell; p13, herring gull and terns;
p15, great spotted woodpecker; p23, skylark; p26, nesting fulmar
with primroses and campion; p32, ammonite and belemnite

Maps by Jeremy Ashcroft

Cover: Whitby Abbey and Harbour by Deryck Hallam

A British Library Cataloguing-in-Publication record
is available for this book

ISBN 1 85568 163 3

Printed by Amadeus Press, Cleckheaton

PUBLISHER'S NOTE
.............................................................................................................................
The information given in this book has been provided in good faith and is intended only
as a general guide. Whilst all reasonable efforts have been made to ensure that details
were correct at the time of publication, the author and Country Publications Ltd
cannot accept any responsibility for inaccuracies. It is the responsibility of individuals
undertaking outdoor activities to approach the activity with caution and, especially if
inexperienced, to do so under appropriate supervision. The activity described in this book
is strenuous and individuals should ensure that they are suitably fit before embarking
upon it. They should carry the appropriate equipment and maps, be properly clothed and
have adequate footwear. They should also take note of weather conditions and forecasts,
and leave notice of their intended route and estimated time of return.

# Contents

# Introduction

To the north and south of Whitby, the hills, moors and dales of the North York Moors National Park finally give way to the North Sea. Before they do, however, they offer the walker one last opportunity to savour the rare beauty of this regal land.

Famous for its historic abbey, often lashed by violent storms and howling gales, Whitby throngs with tourists and holidaymakers during the season. But those seeking more peaceful recreation can easily discover the wealth of fascinating coastal and country walks right on the town's doorstep.

The wonderful sense of space and distance stimulated by tramping the North York Moors is matched only by the liberating experience of exploring the region's spectacular North Yorkshire and Cleveland Heritage Coast on foot. Here, the sights and sounds of the sea assault the senses, diverting the attention by laying bare its greatest riches. Thankfully, the coastline's protected status has enabled it to retain its unique character and culture.

North of Whitby lies Sandsend, with its delightfully spacious 2-mile beach attracting scores of sunbathers and wind-surfers during the summer months. The village marks the starting point for three very pleasant walks in the area, one taking you across country to Kettleness and back via a glorious clifftop stretch of the Cleveland Way, while the other two allow you to discover the pastoral countryside and glorious woodland to the west of Sandsend.

To the south-west of Whitby lies the village of Sleights, representing the start of a most memorable linear walk along a stretch of the 35-mile Esk Valley Walk, which follows this delightful salmon river from its source to the sea at Whitby. Once you have completed the walk, you can return to Sleights on the Esk Valley Railway.

Further west, there is the opportunity to enjoy a short stroll around Glaisdale, while to the south of Whitby you can explore the densely shaded upper reaches of May Beck, taking a gentle stroll between overhanging trees and through tunnels of thick foliage.

# Ugthorpe and Mickleby

**Length of walk: 3¹/₂ miles**
**Start/finish: Ugthorpe village centre. Ugthorpe is west of Whitby**
**Terrain: Mostly field paths across undulating countryside. The walk crosses several becks and some sections of the route can get rather overgrown in summer**

*A pleasant, undemanding walk, rectangular in shape, which links two peaceful villages —Ugthorpe and Mickleby. More of a country ramble than a moorland tramp, the route offers fine views over rolling farmland. There are also occasional coastal vistas.*

Evidence suggests Ugthorpe may well have been a Roman settlement in the 1st century AD. Late in the 18th century, a cache of Roman coins was found in a field near the village. A house on the edge of Ugthorpe was the home of Father Nicholas Postgate, the famous 'Martyr of the Moors', who was persecuted for performing his ministerial duties during the Roman Catholic suppression. Nearby are the remains of a disused windmill, now a private house.

Head east out of the village along Postgate Way, named after Father Postgate, passing the Church of England village hall. A seat comes into view on the left. Just as the road begins to curve to the right, look for a footpath sign on the left and pass through the narrow gap in the hedgerow. Cross a stile and keep ahead, with the field boundary on the left. The distant line of the North Sea can be glimpsed from here.

Veer obliquely right to a stile. Cross two more stiles in quick succession, follow the hedgerow, passing under power lines to drop down the slope. Make for the next stile and cross the Mickleby Beck. Follow the path to the right and left, then head up the slope to a field. Keep the hedge on the right and make for the stile in the bottom corner. Cross a footbridge, heading straight up the field slope. Aim for a gap ahead in the hedgerow, continue across an elongated field to the stile in the top boundary. The buildings of Mickleby can be seen ahead.

Cross the field to a gap between houses and go out to the road via a dog stile. Turn left, pass the White Hart public house and the old Wesleyan chapel and follow the main street. Bear left immediately beyond the Congregational church onto a footpath. Cross the stile, by the entrance to a bungalow, and bear almost immediately right. Cross the field diagonally to a stile in the hedgerow. Turn left onto an enclosed path, veering right after a few yards to a field. Head straight across it, keeping to the left of Pond Farm.

Make for the second of two parallel tracks ahead, swing left and head down to a gate and stile. Follow the track, skirting several fields to a gate. Continue ahead on a grassy path, keeping alongside the hedge as far as its corner. At this point begin to drop down the slope, making for a footbridge concealed among trees. Cross the Mickleby Beck and then head up the slope, curving left alongside a ragged row of trees and bushes. On reaching the ridge of the field, a stile looms into view in the hedgerow ahead.

The path follows the field boundary, offering pleasant views over an unspoilt pastoral landscape. Cross several boundaries and head for a waymark which guides walkers into the field on the left. Pass through a gate and maintain the same direction, with the hedge now on the right. Make for a gate in the field corner and continue on the waymarked path, following it alongside the boundary. The impressive facade of Ugthorpe House is visible away to the right. Bear left at the road, opposite the Black Bull inn, and return to the centre of Ugthorpe, passing 19th-century St Ann's Roman Catholic church.

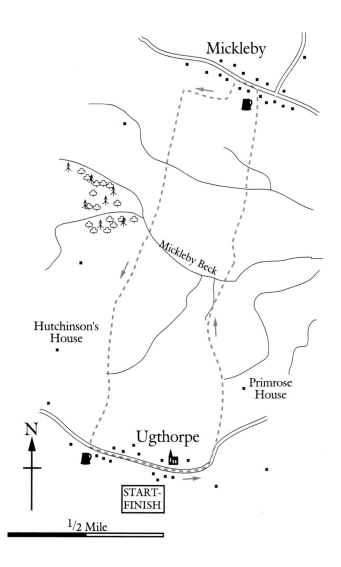

Mickleby

Mickleby Beck

Hutchinson's
House

Primrose
House

Ugthorpe

START-
FINISH

N

1/2 Mile

# Goldsborough Roman Signal Station

**Length of walk:  6 miles**
**Start/finish: Sandsend on the A174 coast road north of Whitby. Use the car park at northern end of the village, by Sandsend Bridge**
**Terrain: After a short spell on the road, steep and quite busy, the walk follows field paths and tracks over rural farmland and along the route of a disused railway**

*This walk combines the natural beauty of the North Yorkshire coastline with a fascinating insight into how the region was defended by the Romans against enemy attack. Climbing briskly towards a breezy headland, the walk makes for Sandsend Ness, skirting the site of a disused alum quarry. The countryside around the signal station may be calm and tranquil now, but this intricately designed defence system would have been a hive of frantic activity during the Occupation, with a constant vigil maintained over the surrounding area.*

With its spacious, sandy beach and protective wall of cliffs, Sandsend has long been a popular holiday base. The sands stretch for over two miles/3.2km, all the way to the west pier by Whitby harbour. Several becks dash down to the sea at Sandsend and the village includes rows of picturesque, honey-coloured cottages. According to some sources, Lewis Carroll took a seaside stroll at Sandsend, inspiring him to write his poem about the Walrus and the Carpenter. The Romans are known to have operated a cement works here during the Occupation.

From the car park by Sandsend Bridge, turn right and walk up the hill, following the A174 as it curves to the right. Bear right just before the National Park boundary sign and join a footpath. A superb view of Sandsend Wyke and the buildings of the village opens up here. Pass

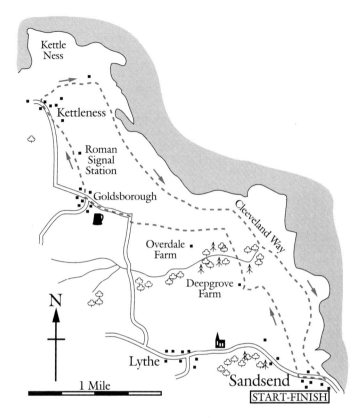

through the gate and keep alongside the fence. Continue beyond the next waymark. Go up the slope and skirt the field by keeping the fence and coast on the right. Cross the stile in the field corner; St Oswald's church at nearby Lythe can be seen over to the left, its spire soaring against the horizon.

Avoiding a concessionary route (denoted by a white arrow), the path runs round the rim of Deep Grove Quarry, once mined for alum but now disused and returning to a state of natural vegetation. Cross two enclosures towards the buildings of Deepgrove Farm. Join a track leading to the farm, then bear right at the sign for Kettleness. Cross a stile and continue towards some woodland. Descend a flight of steps, cross over a beck and take the path as it runs left and right, up the slope; steps make the going a little easier. Cross a stile at the top, bear left and follow the field boundary.

Take the next left-hand track and follow it to Overdale Farm. Pass through a gate and join the next track on a bend. Go straight ahead and turn right at the road. Bear left and walk into the centre of Goldsborough. Pass the village inn and note the amusing sign, depicting a fox and some hounds playing dominoes, drinking and generally enjoying a convivial evening. Follow the road towards Kettleness, bearing right after a short distance into a farmyard.

Veer left and head between the outbuildings to a stile and gate. Go down to the next gate, beyond which are a stile and waymark. Head diagonally across the field towards a solitary cottage, standing out against the sea. This immediate area marks the site of a Roman signal station and beside the footpath is a written and illustrated account of its history.

Goldsborough is one of a series of 4th-century signal stations built along this coast between Flamborough Head and the River Tees. Their key role was to provide the Roman Garrison with advance warning of marauding Scottish or Saxon raiders. Each station conformed to the same design, consisting of a central tower surrounded by a wall enclosing an area 90 metres square.

A beacon, sending signals of fire or drifting smoke from the top of the tower, could be spotted from the next station. The signals were relayed to navy bases in the Tyne and Humber estuaries, and to a cavalry unit at Malton, allowing Roman forces to intercept the invaders. Typically, this strategy was well-planned and effective.

Over 300 coins were found at the Goldsborough site when it was excavated at the end of the First World War. The dates on them indicate the signal station here was occupied between 368 AD and 395 AD. Other evidence suggests that Goldsborough might have been ransacked and later abandoned.

Cross the stile and go diagonally down the field and look for a stile to the right of the disused Chapel of St John the Baptist, famous in this area for its striking patterned roof. Make for the road and turn right. Pass the entrance to Cliff House Farm and follow the lane between the buildings of Kettleness. Look for a sign for the Cleveland Way, bear right and follow the trail over the cliffs towards Sandsend. The path skirts various fields, with the North Sea dominating the view. The church at Lythe, a useful landmark, makes another appearance on this walk.

Having crossed a number of stiles on this stretch of the route, go down some steps, uneven in places, to the route of the former Middlesbrough to Whitby railway. The mouth of a tunnel can be seen on the right here; a sign advises pedestrians to keep out due to roof-fall and subsidence. Turn left and follow the disused trackbed towards Sandsend. When the car park comes into view, take the stepped path on the left.

# Sandsend and Mulgrave Woods

> **Length of walk: 4¹/₂ miles**
> **Start/finish: East Row Beck car park, Sandsend, between Whitby and Staithes. The car park is immediately off the A174, at the entrance to Mulgrave Woods**
> **Terrain: Easy woodland paths, though not waymarked; no steep climbs**

*Delightful walk following permitted paths through broadleaved and conifer woodland. Access to Mulgrave Woods is free of charge, on foot only and is restricted to Saturday, Sunday and Wednesday. The woods are closed completely to walkers during May.*

Picturesque rivulets running down from Mulgrave Woods divide Sandsend into several separate communities which are linked by a bright and breezy promenade lined with hotels, guest houses and apartment buildings. Looking at the bustling seafront and firm sandy beach on a summer day, it is hard to believe that the Romans had a cement works here. In more recent years, between the 17th and 19th centuries, Sandsend was the setting for a thriving alum industry mined from the exposed outcrop of Sandsend Ness. When the mines eventually closed in 1871, a new industry was established in the village, producing a cement strong enough to support a sea wall between tides. This was known as Sandsend Roman Cement.

Make for the gate at the far end of the car park and follow the beckside path away from Sandsend into Mulgrave Woods. In summer the sound of traffic and the playful cries of children soon fade into the distance as you leave the bustling seaside scene behind you and plunge ever deeper into the woodland. Pass a house and timber yard and follow the winding track in a south-westerly direction for nearly 2 miles. Numerous tracks and paths tempt you to leave the main drive, but stay with it as it runs along the north side of East Row Beck valley. The beck should be seen or heard at all times along this stretch.

Mulgrave Woods consist mainly of traditional broadleaved and conifer woodland and thankfully were not cleared as part of the war effort during the First World War, as many similar woods were. Autumn is a perfect time for a stroll here when the rich tints and hues of the leaves create a dazzling picture.

On reaching a clearing, dotted with copper beech, oak and rowan trees, a wooden hut can be seen. Keep right at the fork and then left to a bridge over the beck. Stay on the main track and follow it down below Castle Rigg. At the next main fork, by a seat, veer left for a further half mile. Conifers and a copse of silver birch can be seen on this stretch of the walk. On reaching a cross track, avoid the footbridge on the left and head north by turning right to a second cross track on Castle Rigg.

Bear right here and follow the track for about 500 yards to the site of Mulgrave Castle. Only the sad ruins remain now but this was once an imposing 13th century castle commanding a fine position close to the Yorkshire coast. During the Civil Wars, Mulgrave was held by troops loyal to Charles I before being dismantled by the victorious Parliamentarian forces. Built during the reign of King John by the family of De Mauley, the castle is thought to occupy the site of an earlier Saxon stronghold. According to legend, the giant Wade and his wife Bell were the original inhabitants of this site and are supposedly buried nearby. There is no reference to the Saxon castle in the Domesday Book which suggests that it may have been destroyed by William the Conqueror.

Continue ahead over Castle Rigg and then veer left at the first fork. Turn right at the arched bridge and then swing left. Descend gradually for almost half a mile to the wooden hut and chestnut clearing and then retrace your steps along the main track to the car park where the walk began.

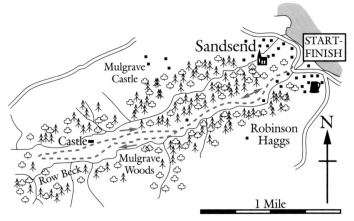

# Sandsend and Dunsley

**Length of walk: 3 miles**
**Start/finish: Sandsend, on the A174 between Whitby and Staithes.**
**Layby on the A174 at the Whitby end of the village; alternatively, park**
**at either of Sandsend's two main car parks off the A174**
**Terrain: Lengthy stretch of minor country lane; field and woodland**
**paths, tracks and drives. Muddy in places, especially under trees**

*A delightful circular walk picking its way inland from Sandsend to the village of Dunsley, then returning to the coast across open farmland and along pretty woodland paths. There are occasional glimpses of the sea along the way.*

Sheltering in the lee of a steep hill, the village of Sandsend boasts one of the best beaches on the Yorkshire coast and from it you can identify the sad ruins of Whitby Abbey standing out on the horizon. The Victorians built a scenic coastal railway at Sandsend and for many years its imposing viaduct was a notable local landmark. Linking Whitby with Middlesbrough, the line eventually closed in the late 1950s.

From the A174 take the road

13

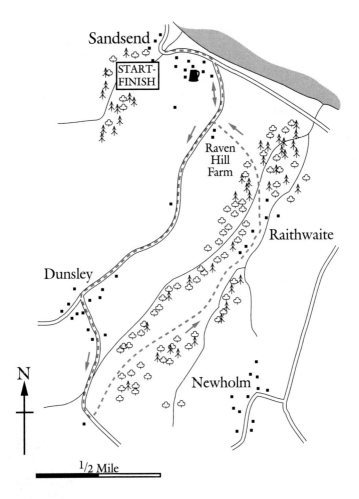

Sandsend

START-FINISH

Raven Hill Farm

Raithwaite

Dunsley

Newholm

N

1/2 Mile

signposted Dunsley, at the Whitby end of Sandsend. Follow Dunsley Lane between grassy banks, climbing quite steeply away from the main road and the beach beyond. Further up, there are spectacular views of Sandsend and its magnificent coastal setting. Pass the buildings of Raven Hill Farm and continue along the winding lane between hedgerows and fences, heading towards Dunsley. Avoid a footpath on the right and soon you reach the village.

Turn left in the centre of Dunsley, signposted Newholm and Whitby, and pass Dunsley Hall Hotel on the left. Head out of the village and down into a wooded dip. A beck can be seen dashing beneath the road and out through the woodland below. Go up the slope and when you break cover from the trees, turn left just before the entrance to Warnbeck Farm Cottages. Follow the path along the edge of a rectangular field and the smooth expanse of the North Sea can just be glimpsed on the far horizon. Pass a gate on the right and walk beneath some power cables. Keep the fence on the right and make for an opening in the hedge. Avoid a path running off to the left to Dunsley and continue straight ahead along a grassy track between fields. Pass through the next boundary gap and head towards a curtain of woodland.

Follow the track as it narrows to become a sunken path running between trees and bracken. Keep on the path as it runs through pretty woodland with a beck seen over on the right, and continue to the edge of a lake. Avoid the path and footbridge on the right and swing left to a wrought iron gate. Follow the grassy path alongside the lake and up ahead is a distinctive neo-classical bridge. Join a tarmac drive and follow it through the grounds of Raithwaite Hall. A large garden and extensive greenhouses can be seen over to the right before you reach the main house. Raithwaite Hall includes tearooms and luxury holiday accommodation. Pass a footpath sign for Sandsend and follow the drive to some cottages.

Turn left at the Sandsend sign and follow the woodland path to a stile. Cross lumpy pasture and scrub and note the views of the sea over to the right. Make for another stile and cross the field to a stile and galvanized gate. Head straight on in the next field, keeping to the right of the outbuildings at Raven Hill Farm. Turn right at the road and return to Sandsend.

# Borrowby

Length of walk: 2¹/₂ miles
Start/finish: Borrowby, north of the A171 between Whitby and Guisborough
Terrain: Field paths, country lanes and tracks; several short ascents

*Short walk exploring undulating countryside in the north-east corner of the North York Moors National Park.*

Borrowby, lying just inside the National Park boundary, is surely one of the most isolated settlements in the North York Moors, with no inn or shop.

Walk north-east through the village, passing Middle Farm and Sycamore Cottage and avoiding a public footpath to Roxby on the left. There are teasing glimpses of the sea at this early stage of the walk. Pass some corrugated barns and farm outbuildings and then bear right at the stile set in the bushes. Once clear of it, pause for a few moments to absorb the glorious view.

Cut by wooded 'wykes' and bays and once the haunt of smugglers, this designated coast, extending for 36 miles between Saltburn-by-the-Sea and Scalby Ness, is distinguished by its soaring cliffs and chain of picturesque fishing villages. The popular holiday resorts of Whitby and Scarborough are the two largest settlements on this stretch of coastline, rich in fossils and minerals.

Veer diagonally right down the field slope, heading for a footpath sign by some bushes and trees. Pass the sign to reach a stile and descend some steps towards power lines. The farm at Low Borrowby can be seen down below. Cross the grass to the road, keeping the house and outbuildings over to the right as you go. Turn right and, avoiding the path running off to the left, follow the narrow, single-track lane as it drops downhill quite steeply. Pass a footpath sign and stile on the left and continue along the lane as it sweeps to the right. Cross a dashing beck via the bridge and then follow the lane as it bends left, climbing between fences and hedges.

Take the next bridleway track on the right and follow it alongside trees and hedgerow. The track becomes steadily steeper on the approach to the farm. On reaching the buildings, look for a gate on the right. Cross the field to a gate in the corner and follow the track to a galvanized gate. Once through it, turn right and go down the field, keeping the fence on the right. Make for a wooden gate and waymark in the bottom corner of the field. Look for a gate down by the trees in the next field and follow a very pleasant woodland path.

Cross a footbridge over a beck and go straight ahead up the grassy slope. Keep right further up, with the fence parallel on the right. Pass a right-angled boundary and then veer off half left, leaving the path that hugs the fence. Go diagonally across the moorland slopes to a stile. Turn right and follow the road back into Borrowby. This final stretch of the walk offers superb views over a rural landscape stretching all the way to the coast.

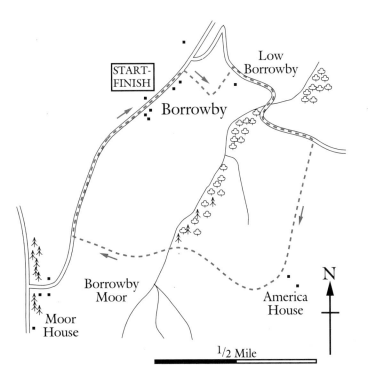

# Glaisdale

**Length of walk: 2¹/₂ miles**
**Start/finish: Glaisdale, south of the A171 between Whitby and Guisborough**
**Terrain: Tracks and paths along the valley floor and across open farmland. Muddy in places, particularly on the shaded stretches near the river. Several short ascents**

*Short walk with pretty views of the River Esk and the undulating countryside of Esk Dale.*

Once an ironstone mining village boasting three blast furnaces, Glaisdale stands at the foot of a narrow, steep-sided dale on the route of the famous 190-mile Coast to Coast Walk which attracts scores of enthusiastic hikers every year. Pioneered by Alfred Wainwright, better known as 'AW' or just simply 'Wainwright', the long-distance trail extends the width of England between St Bees on the Cumbrian west coast and Robin Hood's Bay on the Yorkshire east coast.

The many paved causeways in the area are a permanent reminder of the days when Glaisdale was an important trading centre. Goods were carried by pannier pony and a number of these ancient tracks and paths converge on Beggar's Bridge, a picturesque packhorse bridge spanning the River Esk.

The bridge was built around 1620 by Tom Ferris who later became a successful merchant and Lord Mayor of Hull. As a young man living in Glaisdale, he sought the hand in marriage of Agnes Richardson, daughter of the local squire, who lived on the opposite bank of the unfordable river. To improve his chances with Agnes, young Ferris joined a ship setting out from Whitby to fight the Spanish Armada.

However, the Esk in spate prevented him from bidding farewell to his beloved Agnes, though when he eventually returned to his native Yorkshire, he married his sweetheart and, recalling his thwarted attempts to reach her on the opposite bank, built a bridge across the Esk so that other young lovers need not be parted by the swollen river!

Walk through the centre of Glaisdale, passing rows of stone cottages and terrace houses. Bear left at the telephone box (local traffic only), follow the road round the right-hand bend, pass a seat by the roadside, then bear left by the entrance to a bungalow called 'Wren's Nest'. Go through a kissing gate and head down the track through the beech trees. The River Esk peeps into view far below, creating a glorious picture in any season. However, autumn is probably the best time to appreciate this delightful scene, when the trees conspire to present a rich tapestry of multifarious shades and hues.

Follow the track almost to the water's edge and a stone dwelling can be seen

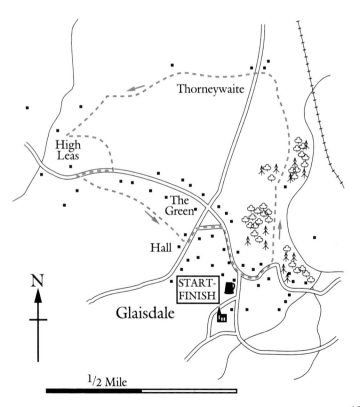

ahead. Take the path to the left of it and climb some steps up through the trees to reach a ladder stile. Continue on a path, muddy at times, cutting between undergrowth, wayside plants and foliage. When you emerge from the trees, there is a striking view of Esk Dale on the right, the river meandering beneath rolling hills and lush pastures. Cross three stiles to reach the gardens of a private house. Follow the right of way round the side of the property and out to the road via a ladder stile.

Turn left for several yards, bearing right to join a tarmac drive which coincides with a public right of way. As you approach the cottage, a well looms into view over to the right. Turn left at the waymark, follow the paved path down to a gate and then go straight on over grass. Avoid a footpath on the left and continue on the grassy path to the next gate. Keep ahead, cutting between grass and bracken and when the track forks, keep left to reach a clear drive. Go straight over towards a bungalow and follow the track round past the front of it.

Pass several properties and when you reach a house and several cottages on the right of the track, bear sharp left and go up the grassy slope to the corner of a wire fence. Walk ahead with the fence on your left and when you reach the curve of a track, bear right and follow it up to the road.

Turn right and look away to the north for a superb view across Esk Dale. Pass the entrance to High Leas and as you reach the village sign for Glaisdale, swing left to join a public bridleway. Cross a ladder stile and then skirt the field, keeping the fence and drystone wall on your left. Maintain the same direction and cross several field boundaries before reaching some farm outbuildings. Go through a gate to the road and turn left. Veer right at the green, where there is a seat, and return to the centre of Glaisdale.

# The Esk Valley Walk

**Length of walk: 5¹/₂ miles**
**Start: Sleights railway station**
**Finish: Egton Bridge railway station on the A169 to the south west of Whitby. Check the times of trains back to Sleights**
**Terrain: Virtually from start to finish this route follows the Esk Valley Walk; a fine mixture of field paths, green lanes and bridleways on the north bank of the Esk**

*There can surely be no finer way of discovering the Esk Valley's numerous delights than by exploring it on foot. This splendid linear walk captures the rare magic of river valley scenery by flirting with the meandering Esk as far as the enchanting village of Egton Bridge. En route there are glorious views across Esk Dale.*

From the car park turn right and follow the A169, crossing the River Esk at the northern end of the village. The bridge here was constructed in 1937 and replaces an earlier structure further downstream, destroyed by floods in 1930. Once across the river, bear left at the sign for Grosmont. Follow the bridleway to Woodlands Nursing Home, with the Esk visible down below on the left.

Pass the nursing home and continue on the drive for about 50 yards. Turn left and follow the paved path down to a gate in the corner. Keep the fence on the right as the path approaches a farmhouse. Bear left at the stile for Grosmont, following the lane as far as a metal gate and a fingerpost on the left. Follow the trod, with glorious views across Esk Dale. Keep to the path alongside and then through trees. Cut across the field towards a wood, pass through a gate to a footbridge, then follow the path up steps and round to the right to a gate on the opposite side of a lane.

Once through the gate, climb steadily between trees and curve right to reach a gate. Skirt two fields by keeping to the right-hand boundary, make for a gate adjacent to a metal gate and now follow the left-hand edge of the field.

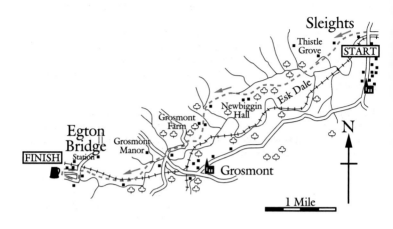

Join a woodland path at the next gate and, beyond the trees, take the track towards Newbiggin Hall Farm.

Cross two stiles and pass the farm buildings. As the track begins to curve right, cross a stile at the sign for Grosmont. Follow the paved path between field boundaries. Pass through a gate, bear left round the edge of a field and continue to another gate. Drop down some steps, descending between trees and undergrowth. Turn left at a junction of paths and head down to a gate.

Join a track, crossing the ford via the footbridge, and follow the green lane through several gates to Grosmont Farm. Continue ahead, eventually reaching the road. Go straight on, passing Priory Park, a residential development, on the left. Turn left at the next junction. Follow the road if intending to visit Grosmont, otherwise bear right after about 100 yards. A sign, positioned in the shadow of a sturdy old beech tree, points towards Egton Bridge. Follow the track alongside the Esk, passing through a gate and beneath the Middlesbrough to Whitby railway line. A cottage soon comes into view ahead; once past it glance up at the gable end.

A sign attached to the wall indicates that this was once a toll road, falling within the jurisdiction of Egton Estates Office. Late-night traffic certainly wasn't encouraged on this route. The gate was closed and locked at 10pm daily. The sign, which is dated August 1948, is in the form of a tariff, listing charges for motor buses, hearses, tractors, lorries, cars and motorcycles.

Pass a bridleway and a footpath as the track cuts through the parkland of Egton Manor, renowned in the area for its Californian redwoods. The fine house can soon be glimpsed through the trees. On reaching the road, turn left, cross the Esk and make for the Horseshoe Inn. The bar boasts a large stuffed trout caught near here in 1913.

Veer right at the entrance and take the path down to the stepping stones. Cross the river, follow the path between houses to the road and turn right. Bear left at the next main junction, pass St Hedda's Roman Catholic church and follow the road to the station at Egton Bridge.

St Hedda's, dating from the 1860s, is closely associated with Father Nicholas Postgate, the rebel Catholic priest who was born at Egton Bridge in the late-16th century and became famous as one of the last of the English martyrs. Postgate took enormous personal risk by continuing to minister to his flock at the height of the Roman Catholic suppression, tramping the moors in all weathers to bring relief and succour to the region's poorest families. But Postgate's luck eventually ran out. After baptizing a child, he was tried at York and later hanged at Tyburn.

# Sneaton

**Length of walk: 2¹/₄ miles**
**Start/finish: Beacon Way, Sneaton, south of Whitby, between the A169
and the A171**
**Terrain: Paved path, field paths, tracks and a stretch of country lane**

*Short walk within sight of Whitby and following part of the delightful, paved
Monk's Walk. Sneaton is famous in this corner of Yorkshire for Beacon
Farm, a mecca for ice cream lovers.*

With the church on your left, walk along beside the village hall and turn left
at the footpath sign for Whitby. Follow the track alongside farm
outbuildings to a gate and here the historic buildings of Whitby can be seen
defining the horizon.

The abbey also became the subject of enemy bombardment when German
warships attacked it during the First World War. Next door to the abbey lies the
church of St Mary, which is closely associated with Count Dracula. Bram
Stoker's classic story refers to the graveyard as being one of Dracula's haunts.

Go through a gate and join a paved path known as the Monk's Walk. The
monks and nuns of nearby Whitby Abbey owned extensive land in the area
and quite possibly used this path to reach outlying farmland – hence the
name. Follow the path between trees and hedgerows, cutting across a most
attractive pastoral landscape. Eventually the path cuts down through the
trees, bending left by a stile. Avoid it and keep to the paved path through the
woodland, crossing a footbridge over the Shawn Riggs Beck further down.

Follow the path hard by the beck to the next footbridge, then head up the
bank out of the trees to follow a broad bridleway between hedgerows. Once
again there are good views over to Whitby. Turn right at a galvanized gate
and follow the footpath across the field to a stile in the boundary, aiming
slightly right in the next field. Cross a second stile and keep to the right of
some power lines. Make for a third stile in the right-hand corner of the top

boundary hedge. Follow the path with the hedge on your immediate left, pass a gate and continue as far as Bennison House Farm.

Cross a stile in front of the farm outbuildings and turn right. Walk down the track past the farmhouse and cut between trees and hedgerows. Further on, you will see a sign for oncoming traffic – 'Bennison House Farm – representatives by appointment only'. Immediately beyond the sign, the track becomes a metalled lane. Follow it as it winds through the gently rolling countryside, passing a solitary house, 'Bennison View', on the right.

Just beyond it is a glorious view of Sneaton's rural setting. The village church is visible, serving as a useful landmark, and away in the distance is the smooth expanse of the sea merging almost imperceptibly with the sky. Drop down through a tunnel of trees and pass a stile and footpath on the right. Head up the next slope and follow Beacon Way back into Sneaton, passing the Wilson Arms and Beacon Farm on the right.

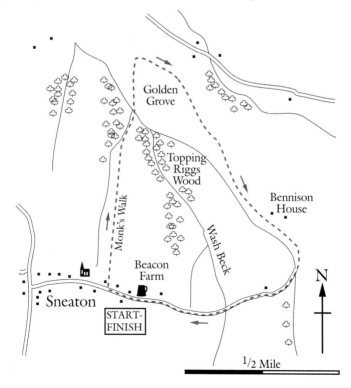

# Littlebeck and Iburndale

**Length of walk: 4¹/₂ miles**
**Start/Finish: Littlebeck: parking spaces at the village hall. The village
is south of Whitby, between the A171 and the A169**
**Terrain: Some road walking, steep in places, rough moorland, green
lanes and field paths, meadows, woodland and stepping stones**

*Buried deep among rolling hills and wooded valleys, Littlebeck is one of
those delightful little hamlets that you stumble upon by accident. The walk
is equally well-hidden, adding to its unique charm. Beginning with a stiff
climb out of the valley, the route heads over open moorland and farmland
before reaching Iburndale, a small village adjacent to the better-known
Sleights. From Iburndale, the walk makes for the banks of the magical Little
Beck, a delight in any season. The path darts playfully back and forth across
the water until at length it makes for the verdant slopes of the valley,
returning to the road at Littlebeck.*

The scene at Littlebeck is serene and tranquil today, but until the 19th
century the area to the south of this tiny community was a centre for alum
mining, an industry which flourished here for 300 years. From the car park
turn right and follow the road to the junction. Bear right and follow Lousy
Hill Lane (signposted: local traffic only). Climb steeply between trees and
hedgerows; the openings and gateways on the right
provide superb views across Scarry Wood towards
the valley of the May Beck and Fylingdales.
Pass the entrance to Moorside Farm and now
the lane swings right. Turn left after about
175 yards to join a bridleway. Follow the
path as it cuts through the bracken,
shoulder-high in places at the height of
summer. On reaching a track, beyond
some trees and scrub, turn left and head
for Moor House Farm.

Veer right before the outbuildings and keep following the bridleway. Keep right at the first fork, then veer left at the second and follow a narrow path towards some trees. Cut through the wood, emerging from the trees and soon veering left at the next fork. Follow the path between trees and bracken to the road.

Turn right and on the left is a glorious view over the Little Beck. Follow the road to a sign for Dean Hall and turn left, taking the lane down past the farm outbuildings and cottages. Pass a house called 'Sunnymead' and follow Tom

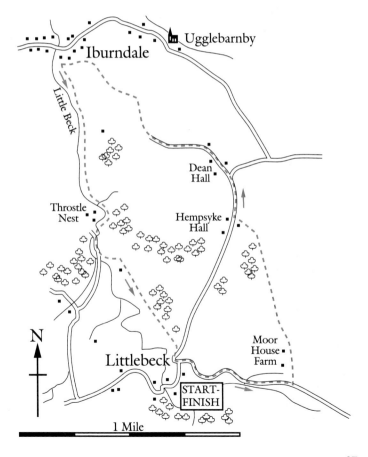

Bell Lane across country. Avoid a track on the left, pass a gateway and continue on a narrow path, following it over some paving stones. Pass another gate and, 30 yards beyond it, is a stile in the left-hand boundary.

Cross the field by veering slightly right to a hedgerow at the bottom. Cross the stile and head diagonally right across the field to a stile in the bottom right corner. Bear right in the next field and make for a stile and gateway. Pass under some power lines, making for a gate to the right of some trees. Curve to the left in the next field, pass through a gate on the far side and bear immediately left through the undergrowth to a stile by a metal gate.

Follow the path alongside private gardens on the outskirts of Iburndale, cross a drive by the entrance to Zetland House and go through a kissing gate on the left. Follow the paved path alongside a paddock and the Little Beck.

Cross a stile and continue between fields and woodland. Soon the path reaches a delightfully-shaded reach of the chattering Little Beck. In fine weather, beams of sunlight flood this quiet spot, filtering between the branches of the overhanging trees to dance on the water. Turn left here and follow the sometimes slippery, rock-strewn bank to a stile. Cross the field, passing under power lines again. There is no direct access to the water's edge on this stretch. Instead, the path crosses fields and meadows, running parallel to the beck.

Eventually, a ladder-stile creeps into view in the corner of the field. Turn left and follow the beck to a footbridge where the boughs of the surrounding trees reach down, almost touching the water. Cross over, bear left and keep going towards Littlebeck at the sign. Pass over the beck via some concrete stepping stones, follow the bank and return to the opposite bank at the next crossing point. Join a road, recrossing the beck, and pass a footbridge on the right. On reaching the ford, take the footpath up the track towards Low Farm.

When the drive bends right, go straight ahead to a stile. Cross several more stiles, with enclosures on the right, and turn right. Keep the fence, hedge and farm outbuildings on the right and make for a stile up ahead. Continue with a hedgerow on the left, crossing several field boundaries to join a woodland track. Turn right at the road and return to the car park.

# May Beck and Falling Foss

> **Length of walk:** 4³/₄
> **Start/finish:** May Beck car park. Access is from the B1416 which links
> the A169 and the A171 south of Whitby
> **Terrain:** This moderate walk enjoys plenty of woodland paths and
> heather moorland. Several short ascents

*Sneaton Forest and the May Beck valley offer an excellent network of paths
and tracks for those in search of peace and solitude. Moments from its start,
this walk plunges deep into a silent land of conifer plantations and bracken-
covered glades. The route skirts the heathery expanses of Fylingdales Moor
before taking shelter among stands of trees and clumps of bracken. Each
season reveals something new and surprising on this walk, but one feature
which remains reassuringly timeless is Falling Foss, one of the North York
Moors National Park's most treasured landmarks, cascading deep among
the trees that overhang the May Beck.*

Sneaton Forest forms one of the seven main blocks of the North Riding
Forest Park. This part of the North York Moors was once densely wooded
with a wide variety of broadleaved trees cloaking the sheltered valley.
Several of these native species survive from the earliest days of settlement
in the area, most probably during the Bronze Age.

Trees were later felled for farming and by the Middle Ages large flocks of
sheep, many of them owned by the monasteries, grazed the hills, preventing
regrowth and regeneration of the forest. Gradually rough moorland took the
place of the trees, changing the appearance and character of the area so
dramatically that today it is hard to believe these open upland tracts were
once thickly afforested. Among the tree species to be found here are
lodgepole pine and Sitka spruce. Timber from Sneaton Forest goes mainly
for paper pulp and chipboard.

Leave the car park by turning right onto a track, pass a sign (No unauthorised vehicles), and further up the slope, look back for a lovely view of the May Beck valley. When the track swings right, take the signposted path running off to the left. Cross the footbridge, avoid the turning on the left and continue ahead on the grassy path. Pass through a kissing gate and follow the course of the chattering May Beck, with banks of bracken and the trees of Sneaton Forest conspiring to engulf the walk. On reaching a signpost, bear right to reach a clear woodland track.

Turn left and when the track curves to the right, bear left to join a waymarked path, running between the trees. Cross a forest drive and continue through dense, silent woodland to the junction by the remains of John Bond's Sheep House.These stone enclosures were used by shepherd John Bond, who stayed here while guarding his flock.

Bear right and a footpath sign is visible about 80 yards away on the edge of the moorland. Cross a footbridge towards the signpost and then follow the path as it skirts the moor. Pass through a kissing gate, then stride out across the carpet of heather, a dazzling picture in summer. Merge with another path and go straight on over Shooting House Rigg. The size and scale of Sneaton Forest, away to the left, can be absorbed on this exposed stretch of the walk. Keep the line of trees as a useful landmark. Now and again, the wind carries the hooting of trains on the North York Moors Railway.

Look for a right of way sign up ahead after some time. On reaching a junction of paths, go straight ahead. The path is not clearly defined on this next stretch, partly obscured by the carpet of heather. In places, it disappears completely. However, there is a wall a short distance to the left. Walk ahead, parallel to the wall, and look for the next signpost, visible against the skyline. On reaching it, turn left through the kissing gate and follow the path across Sneaton Low Moor, curving to the right after about 200 yards. Turn sharp left after about 100 yards and follow the indistinct path across the moorland. Aim to the left of the woodland ahead. Traffic can sometimes be seen on the minor road leading to the car park at May Beck.

Merge with another path and look for the rooftops of a farmstead at New May Beck. On reaching the road, turn left and follow it round to the right. Turn right where the road bears sharp left and follow the waymarked path down to a footbridge. Bear left through a gate and keep to the path as it cuts between woodland and bracken. Head up the slope and alongside a field boundary fence. Cross a stile into a field and keep the boundary on the left.

Head for the far end of the field and join a track, following it between fields and woodland to a stile leading onto a lane. Turn left, passing the entrance

Newton House

Foss Farm

May Beck

New May Beck

Old May Beck

START-FINISH

Standing Stone
Old Wife's Neck

Sneaton
High
Moor

N

1/2 Mile

to Newton House and farm. Pass a parking area for Falling Foss on the left and continue on the lower track (signposted Falling Foss). The sound of rushing water is audible now. Descend between the trees and take the path running off half right, down to the waterfall. Falling Foss, enclosed by beech and birch, plunges 30 feet over a resistant ledge of rock, and is particularly spectacular after a spell of heavy rain. Adjacent Midge Hall was once a keeper's cottage and later a museum; its shaded woodland setting is superb, though the building itself has long been derelict.

Returning to the track, continue down through trees and across May Beck. Pass a signpost for the Coast to Coast walk on the left and keep on the track as it rises quite steeply through the trees. Turn left at the next footpath, after about 100 yards and follow it through the woodland. Pass a seat and then turn left at the next junction. Take the next path on the left and follow it round to the right, passing a stone cottage. Follow the track as it cuts through the trees and undergrowth and soon the car park at May Beck edges into view.